DOG

SOCK

MIRROR

DRUM

for Betsy

—L.C.E.

COPYRIGHT © 2012 BY LISA CAMPBELL ERNST

ALL RIGHTS RESERVED / CIP DATA IS AVAILABLE.

PUBLISHED IN THE UNITED STATES 2012 BY

🍎 BLUE APPLE BOOKS

515 VALLEY STREET, MAPLEWOOD, NJ 07040

WWW.BLUEAPPLEBOOKS.COM

FIRST EDITION 05/12

PRINTED IN GUANDONG, CHINA

ISBN: 978-1-60905-189-1

1 3 5 7 9 10 8 6 4 2

LISA CAMPBELL ERNST

HOW THINGS WORK IN THE HOUSE

BLUE APPLE

HOW DOES A
BANANA
WORK?

A **BANANA** is a sweet, creamy fruit you peel to eat.

fruit

When we eat a banana, our bodies get important vitamins and minerals.

peel

Bananas grow in bunches on tree-sized herbs in places where it is very hot.

Some people rub the inside of a banana skin on mosquito bites to ease the itch.

Banana leaves are used to make rope, rugs, and even fancy kimonos.

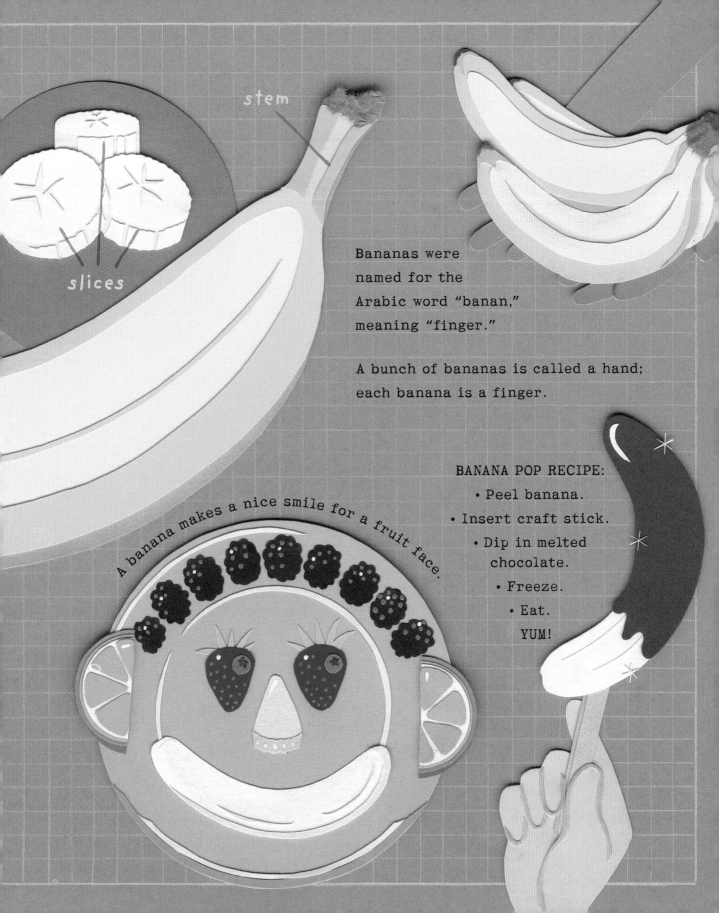

stem

slices

Bananas were
named for the
Arabic word "banan,"
meaning "finger."

A bunch of bananas is called a hand;
each banana is a finger.

A banana makes a nice smile for a fruit face.

BANANA POP RECIPE:
- Peel banana.
- Insert craft stick.
- Dip in melted
  chocolate.
- Freeze.
- Eat.
  YUM!

A **SPOON** is a tool for scooping, stirring, measuring, and eating.

HOW DOES A
SPOON
WORK?

When a spoon is used for stirring, it moves the ingredients around, mixing them together.

Measuring spoons come in different sizes to add just the right amount of an ingredient.

tip

bowl

heel

To make a cool catapult:

tape
block of wood
paint stir stick

plastic spoon

Load the spoon with a mini marshmallow and see how far you can make it sail!

The spoonbill bird scoops up fish
and shrimp with its spoon-shaped bill.

All around the world,
amazing music is made by
tapping spoons together.

handle

Check out your reflection
in a shiny metal spoon:
On the side that curves
toward you (called convex),
you look right side up.

On the side that
curves away from you
(called concave),
you look upside down!

Plastic
spoons make
good puppets.

HOW DOES A FISH WORK?

A **FISH** is an animal that lives in water and swims.

Lateral line that senses motion, pressure, and sound

caudal fins

A fish swims by moving its body and tail back and forth. Oily scales help the fish slip through the water smoothly.

scales that cover the body like a suit of armor

anal fins

Fish need plenty of cool, clean water to stay healthy. In an aquarium, a filter keeps the water clean, and an air pump replaces oxygen.

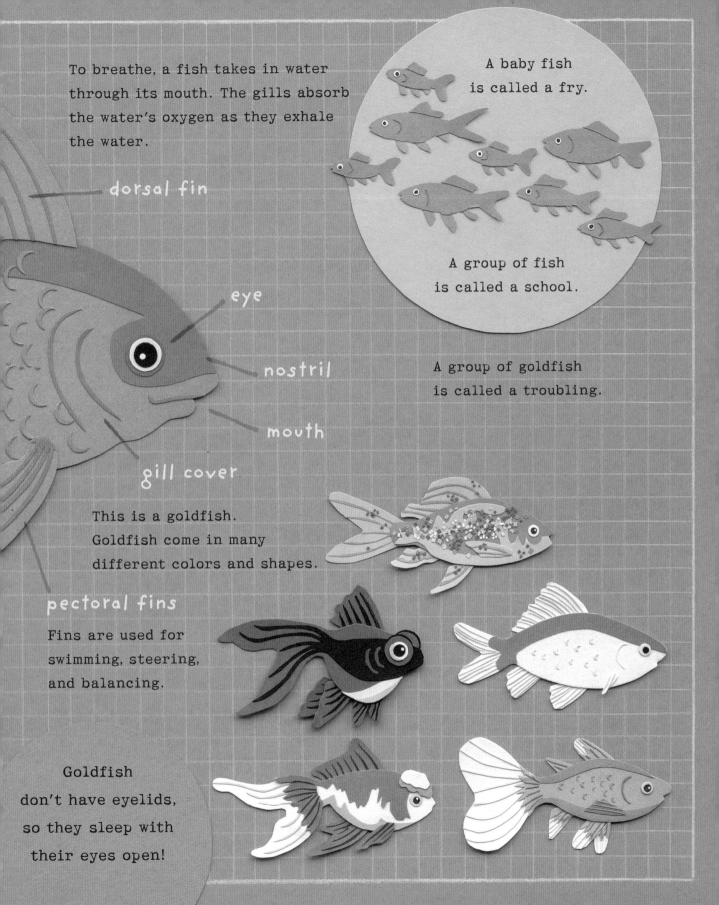

To breathe, a fish takes in water through its mouth. The gills absorb the water's oxygen as they exhale the water.

dorsal fin

A baby fish is called a fry.

A group of fish is called a school.

eye

nostril

A group of goldfish is called a troubling.

mouth

gill cover

This is a goldfish. Goldfish come in many different colors and shapes.

pectoral fins

Fins are used for swimming, steering, and balancing.

Goldfish don't have eyelids, so they sleep with their eyes open!

handle

soft tips
to make
brushing
gentle

bristles
that scrub teeth

head
that holds
the bristles

toothpaste
that helps remove food,
kill germs, and add fluoride

A **TOOTHBRUSH** is a small brush used to clean teeth.

When you brush your teeth and gums, a film of bacteria called plaque is scrubbed off. The acid in plaque can eat holes—called cavities—in your teeth.

HOW DOES A
TOOTHBRUSH
WORK?

tooth
gums
gums
root

Long ago, toothbrushes were made from feathers and wild hog hair.

Electric toothbrushes use batteries to move the bristles.

A **MIRROR** is a special kind of glass that shows a reflection.

smooth, clear glass

coating of metal or paint that protects the silver

shiny, silver metal that bounces the light back

Because they are both smooth and shiny, mirrors are able to show what's in front of them. This image is called a reflection.

If the glass is wavy, the image will be wavy, too.

Mirrors create the beautiful designs in kaleidoscopes.

In telescopes, mirrors reflect light to allow us to see far into outer space.

Socks are usually knit from yarn, either by machines or by hand.

leg

toe

instep

foot

cuff

gusset

heel

HOW DOES A
SOCK
WORK?

A SOCK is a woven covering worn on feet.

Socks cushion your feet inside your shoes.

In cold weather, socks keep your feet warm by holding in your body's heat. That's called thermal energy.

In hot weather, socks absorb the sweat from your feet, keeping them more comfortable.

Japanese tabi socks are made to wear with sandals.

SOCK PUPPET

HOW DOES A
SOCK MONKEY
WORK?

A **SOCK MONKEY** is a stuffed monkey made out of socks.

Here's how the socks get cut up to make a monkey:

body

hat

tail

arms

legs

ears

mouth

Hand-sewn sock monkeys often have a unique, one-of-a-kind look.

Sock monkeys were first made in America during the **1930s**, a time when many people didn't have money for store-bought toys.

A **CRAYON** is a waxy stick used for drawing and coloring.

HOW DOES A CRAYON WORK?

tip

paper wrapper

As a crayon is used, it becomes shorter.

Taping crayons together makes a multicolored design.

Tear the paper wrapper off to expose more of the crayon.

When you move a crayon across a piece of paper, colored wax rubs off onto the paper. The harder you press, the stronger the color.

The artist and inventor Leonardo da Vinci wrote about drawing with wax crayons 500 years ago!

Crayola

blue

name of color

Put a leaf or key under your paper to make a print by rubbing a crayon lightly over the top.

A **STAPLER** is a small machine that bends wire to fasten papers together.

hammer that pushes the front staple out and into the papers

arm that is pressed down

staple before bending

staple after bending

staples lined up for action

anvil

spring that pulls the pusher forward

pusher that pushes the staples forward

crimp area that bends the staple on the back side of the pages.

TO STAPLE:
- insert paper between the anvil and hammer.
- Press down arm.
- Hear *kaCHUNKa* sound.
- Release.

A zigzag-folded paper with a staple at one end makes a fan.

By stapling pages together along one side, you can make a book.

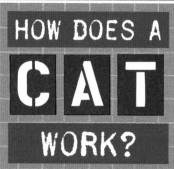

HOW DOES A CAT WORK?

A **CAT** is a small house pet with soft fur.

Cats like to hunt and pounce on things that move— like toys and toes!

A baby cat is called a kitten.

tail
for balance

A cat rubs its body against things to say, "This is mine."

strong legs
for jumping
and pouncing

Cats love to climb in boxes and bags!

Cats talk by meowing.

whiskers
that help feel
surroundings

ears
that turn
to track noises

A cat's purr sounds
like a low rumble
coming from its throat.
Cats purr when they
are happy, and to calm
themselves when they
are upset.

eyes
that see even when
it's nearly dark

Cats like to "sharpen" their
claws by scuffing off an outside
dull layer, revealing a new sharp
claw inside.

paws
that are padded
and silent,
with claws
that slide in
and out

A cat's tongue feels rough because
it is covered with little hooks.
When a cat licks itself to keep clean,
the hooks brush the fur at the same time.

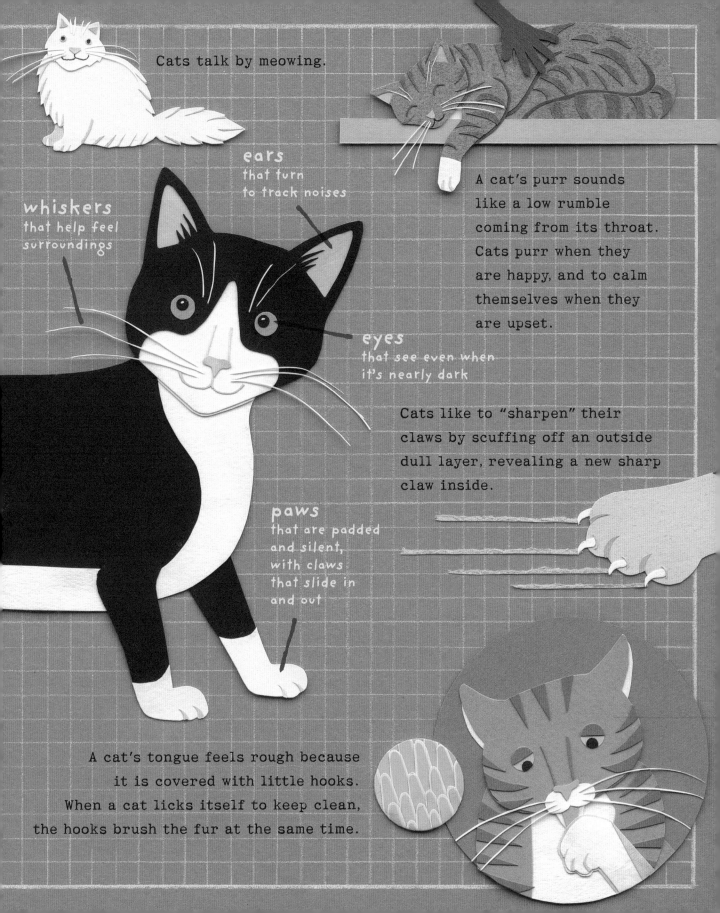

HOW DO SCISSORS WORK?

four
fingers
go here

shanks

screw

joint
area

handles

thumb
goes here

When scissor handles
are pulled apart,
the blades open. As the handles
are pushed together, the blades close,
cutting as
they slide
together.

blade

blade

cutting edges

A pair of **SCISSORS**
is a tool used for cutting.

Fold a paper circle as shown,
then cut a design to make
a snowflake.

Some
scissors have
fancy blades to cut
patterns.

To make
a garland,
fold a long strip
of paper like an
accordion and
cut a design that
allows the folds
to stay connected.

Glue works because even things that might seem smooth— like paper— really have teeny, tiny holes and cracks in them.

GLUE is a gooey, thick liquid that sticks things together.

GLUE
BOTTLE

glue
inside

Putting glue between two pieces of paper causes the glue to ooze into those tiny spaces. When the glue dries, the two surfaces are stuck together.

paper
glue
paper

cap
that screws up to open and allow glue out, down to close and keep air out

Different types of glue are used to help make everything from shoes to cars.

A GLUE RECIPE:
- $\frac{1}{2}$ cup flour
- $\frac{1}{4}$ cup water
- Mix well. Glue!

GLUE
STICK

cap
that keeps
air out

A collage is made by gluing small bits of paper or other things onto a larger surface to make a design or picture. The illustrations for this book are collages.

HOW DOES A SANDWICH WORK?

Sandwich equation: bread + filling + bread

top slice of bread

tomatoes

lettuce

cheese

mustard

bottom slice of bread

meat

Pita bread is round and hollow, perfect for holding sandwich ingredients.

A **SANDWICH** is made of bread and a filling.

A favorite sandwich is the peanut butter and jelly sandwich, sometimes called a PB&J.

Sandwiches are eaten with your hands. Always hold a sandwich on the top and bottom to keep it together.

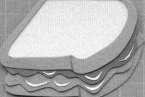

Ice cream between two cookies makes an ice cream sandwich.

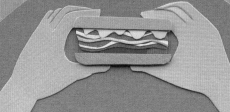

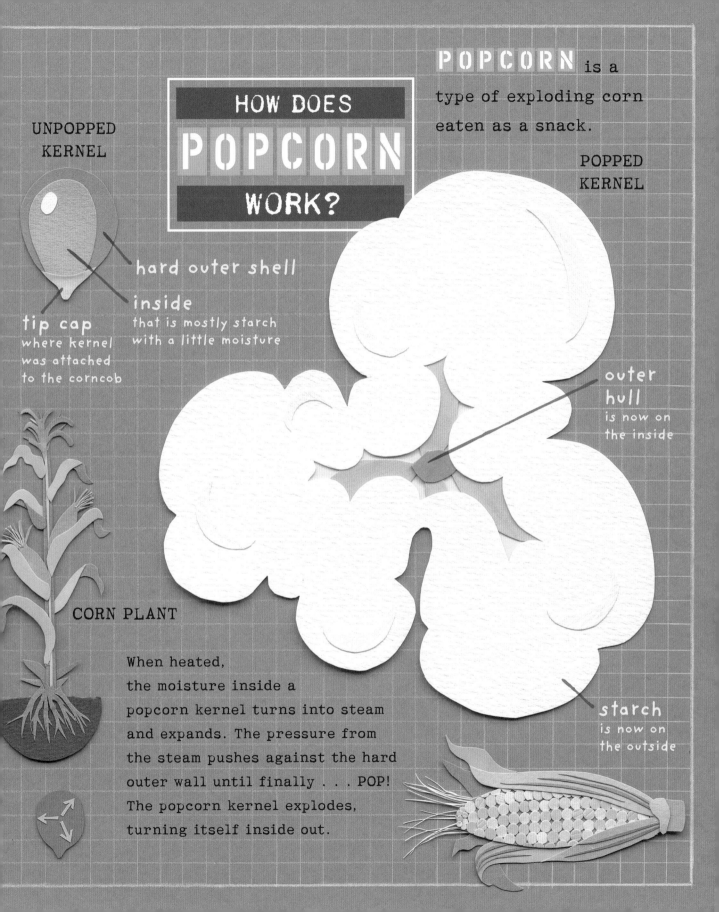

HOW DOES POPCORN WORK?

POPCORN is a type of exploding corn eaten as a snack.

UNPOPPED KERNEL

POPPED KERNEL

hard outer shell

inside
that is mostly starch
with a little moisture

tip cap
where kernel
was attached
to the corncob

outer hull
is now on
the inside

CORN PLANT

starch
is now on
the outside

When heated,
the moisture inside a
popcorn kernel turns into steam
and expands. The pressure from
the steam pushes against the hard
outer wall until finally . . . POP!
The popcorn kernel explodes,
turning itself inside out.

HOW DOES A STRAW WORK?

BENDY STRAW

CRAZY STRAW

wall

Everything on Earth has air pressing against it. When you suck the air out of a straw, the liquid is pushed up the straw by the air that is still pressing on the liquid outside the straw. That's called a vacuum.

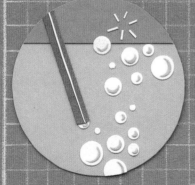

Blowing through a straw in liquid creates air bubbles.

Lei made of straws, paper, and string.

A **STRAW** is a tube used for drinking.

Put a straw in a glass of liquid. Place your finger over the top opening of the straw and lift it out. The liquid will stay inside the straw.

Why? When your finger is over the opening, it stops the air pressure from above. The air pressing up from below holds the liquid in.

The paper wrapping of a straw can be turned into a rocket by blowing it off with a puff of air.

When you move your finger off, the liquid pours out because you've allowed the air to reenter the straw and push it out.

Butterflies have a type of straw called a proboscis that they use to reach deep into flowers and suck out nectar.

A **KAZOO**

is a musical instrument that is played by humming into it.

HOW DOES A KAZOO WORK?

small end
that allows air and sound out

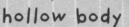

hollow body
that increases volume of humming as sound waves bounce around inside

membrane
made of waxy film that vibrates when sound waves reach it, creating a buzzing sound

hole
that allows most of the sound out

turret

Moving your hand on and off the turret makes a "wah-wah" sound.

larger end
that goes in your mouth

If you can hum, you can play a kazoo.

Wax paper wrapped around a comb makes a simple kazoo.

A **DRUM** is a musical instrument that is played by hitting it.

drumhead
that vibrates when hit, causing the air around it to vibrate, creating sound

Drums are usually played with hands or sticks.

rim
that holds the drumhead in place

tension rod
to adjust the tightness of the drumhead

Drums can make different sounds. The tighter the drumhead is stretched, the higher the sound. The looser the drumhead, the lower the sound.

hollow shell
that traps sound waves— as the sound waves bounce around inside, the sound becomes louder

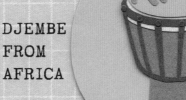

DJEMBE FROM AFRICA

A bucket turned upside down makes a great drum.

BONGO FROM CUBA

A **DOG** is a loyal, playful animal that comes in many shapes and sizes.

ears
that can hear very faint sounds, especially high, squeaky sounds

eyes
that see moving things very well, but don't see many colors

nose
that gives a dog its strongest sense, smell—a thousand times stronger than ours

collar and tag
with information to help a dog get back home if it is lost

A baby dog is called a puppy.

A dog's sense of smell is so powerful that dogs can tell people apart by sniffing them.

A dog's nose print is one-of-a-kind, like a human's fingerprint.

If a dog is hot, it cools off by sticking out its tongue and panting!

Dogs bark when they are excited.

tail

A dog's tail gives clues to its mood. When scared, a dog tucks its tail between its legs. A wagging tail usually means a dog is happy, but it can also mean the dog is stressed or unsure about what what's happening.

fur
that protects a dog's skin from cold, rain, and hot sun, called a "coat"

Some dogs are trained for important jobs. They might help a person who has difficulty moving around, or find people who are lost.

A dog's fur can be long or short, smooth, fluffy, or curly. Mexican Hairless dogs have almost no hair!

SOAP is used for washing and cleaning.

HOW DOES SOAP WORK?

BAR OF SOAP

LIQUID SOAP

SOAP MOLECULE
Soap is made of teeny, tiny bits called molecules.

the head is attracted to water

the tail is attracted to oil, but rejects water

Dirt sticks to the oils on our skin. When we wash with soap and water, one end of the soap molecules latches onto the dirty oils on our skin.

The other end latches onto the water as it swooshes past, carrying off the dirty oils with the water.

As you rub your hands together, the mixture of soap and water traps pockets of air, making bubbles.

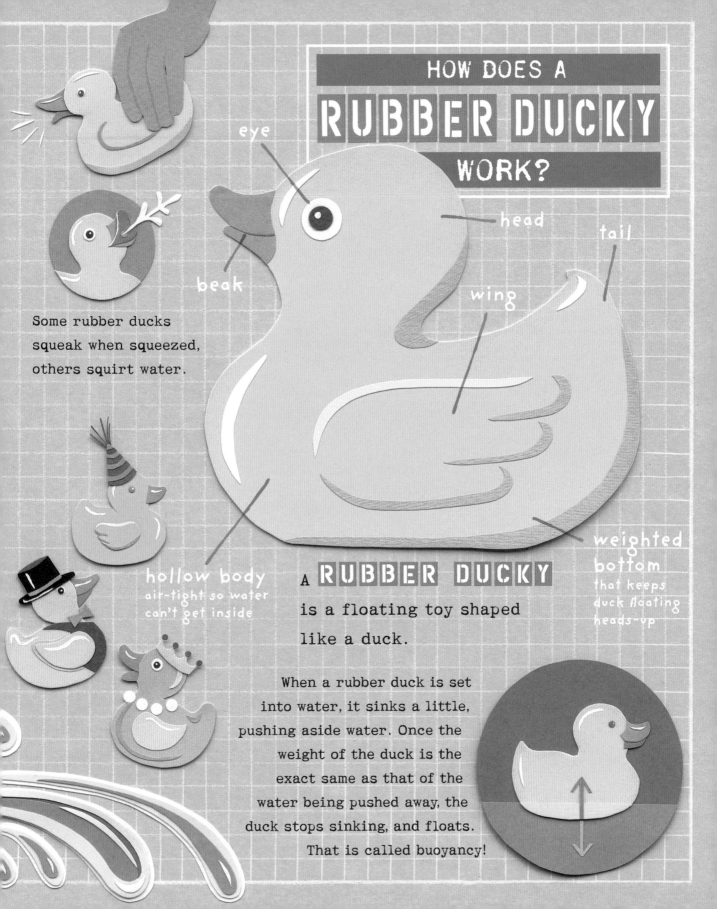

HOW DOES A RUBBER DUCKY WORK?

eye

head

tail

beak

wing

Some rubber ducks squeak when squeezed, others squirt water.

A **RUBBER DUCKY** is a floating toy shaped like a duck.

hollow body
air-tight so water can't get inside

weighted bottom
that keeps duck floating heads-up

When a rubber duck is set into water, it sinks a little, pushing aside water. Once the weight of the duck is the exact same as that of the water being pushed away, the duck stops sinking, and floats. That is called buoyancy!

HOW DOES A
PIGGY BANK
WORK?

A **PIGGY BANK** is a container shaped like a pig, which is used for saving money.

slot
for sliding money in

Putting your money in a piggy bank is one way to save for the future.

ears

snout

To drop money into a piggy bank, turn your coins so they line up with the opening.

plug
that keeps money from falling out

Fold paper money so it can slide through the slot.